GRACEFUL AGEING

SWAMI TEJOMAYANANDA

Central Chinmaya Mission Trust

First Edition - September 2009 - January 2013 - 10,000 copies
Revised Edition - April 2019 - 2,500 copies

Published by:
Chinmaya Prakashan
The Publications Division of
Central Chinmaya Mission Trust
Sandeepany Sadhanalaya,
Saki Vihar Road, Powai, Mumbai - 400 072, India.
Tel.: +91-22-2803 4900
Email: ccmtpublications@chinmayamission.com
Website: www.chinmayamission.com

Distribution Centre in USA:
Chinmaya Mission West
Publications Division,
560 Bridgetown Pike, Langhorne, PA 19053, USA
Tel.: 1-888-CMW-READ, (215) 396-0390 Fax: (215) 396-9710
Email: publications@chinmayamission.org
Website: www.chinmayapublications.com

Illustrations: Brahmacharini Nivedita Chaitanya
Book Design: Radhika Chopra

Printed by: Parksons Graphics, Mumbai.

ISBN: 978-81-7597-462-3

Transliteration and Pronunciation Guide

In the book, Devanagari characters are transliterated according to the scheme adopted by the International Congress of Orientalists at Athens in 1912. In it one fixed pronunciation value is given to each letter; f, q, w, x and z are not called to use. According to this scheme:

Devanagari	Transliteration	Sounds Like	Devanagari	Transliteration	Sounds Like
अ	a	son	ढ्	ḍh	adhesive*
आ	ā	father	ण्	ṇ	under*
इ	i	different	त्	t	tabla
ई	ī	feel	थ्	th	thumb
उ	u	full	द्	d	this
ऊ	ū	boot	ध्	dh	Gandhi
ऋ	ṛ	rhythm*	न्	n	nose
ॠ	ṝ	**	प्	p	pen
ऌ	ḷ	**	फ्	ph	phantom*
ए	e	evade	ब्	b	boil
ऐ	ai	delight	भ्	bh	abhor
ओ	o	core	म्	m	mind
औ	au	now	य्	y	yes
क्	k	calm	र्	r	right
ख्	kh	khan	ल्	l	love
ग्	g	gate	व्	v	very
घ्	gh	ghost	श्	ś	shut
ङ्	ṅ	ankle*	ष्	ṣ	sugar
च्	c	chuckle	स्	s	simple
छ्	ch	witch*	ह्	h	happy
ज्	j	justice	ं	ṁ	improvise
झ्	jh	Jhansi	ः	ḥ	**
ञ्	ñ	banyan	क्ष्	kṣ	action
ट्	ṭ	tank	त्र्	tr	three*
ठ्	ṭh	**	ज्ञ्	jñ	gnosis
ड्	ḍ	dog	ऽ	’	a silent ‘a’

* These letters don’t have an exact English equivalent. An approximation is given here.

** These sounds cannot be approximated in English words.

Whatafool you are!
You don't know where
these roads go??
MAP
Maybe but I'm not lost! You say you are wise but you
are lost. You say I'm a fool, but I'm not lost!
I'm here where I should be!!

CONTENTS

Chapter 5: THE VAIRĀGYA OF VĀNAPRASTHA

Chapter 6: THE BLISS OF SANNYĀSA

PREFACE

Graceful Ageing is a compilation of a series of discourses delivered by Pūjya Swami Tejomayananda at Sandeepany Sadhanalaya Mumbai, in June 2008. He communicated the art of graceful ageing with an ease that makes learning simple and structured for us.

The Central Chinmaya Vanaprastha Samsthan (CCVS), Chinmaya Mission's Vedānta forum for senior citizens, regularly organizes talks on topics relevant to the elderly, such as healthy living, disease prevention, constructive activities, personal, social, and financial planning and management, and psychological well-being. It was thus, a great honour to have Pūjya Swami Tejomayananda conduct an enlightening spiritual camp on '*Graceful Ageing,*' organized by CCVS.

Chinmaya Prakashan
Publications Divn. of CCMT

September 2009

CHINMAYA MISSION

Chinmaya Mission® was established in India in 1953 by devotees of Param Pūjya Swami Chinmayananda. They formed the nucleus of a spiritual renaissance movement that now encompasses a wide range of spiritual, educational and charitable activities, ennobling the lives of thousands in India and outside its borders. Administered by Central Chinmaya Mission Trust in Mumbai, India, the Mission is now headed by Pūjya Swami Swaroopananda.

Following the Vaidika teacher-taught tradition (Guru-śiṣya paramparā), Chinmaya Mission makes available the ageless wisdom of Vedānta, (the knowledge of the one Reality), and provides the tools to realize that wisdom in one's life. 'To give maximum happiness to the maximum number for the maximum time' is the tenet that drives Mission workers to uplift humanity beyond selfish and sectarian attitudes and activities. Each person's gain is manifold – personal growth, heightened efficiency, contentment, and the ability to live with others in peace and harmony.

For more information, visit www.chinmayamission.com or read *Chinmaya Mission: Transforming Lives.*

Param Pūjya Swami Chinmayananda, founder of Chinmaya Mission, taught spirituality as the art of living. Through jñāna-yoga (the path of knowledge), he emphasized the balance of head and heart, with selfless work, study and meditation as the corner stones of spiritual practice.

Not satisfied by worldly aspirations or his degrees in literature and law, Balakrishna Menon pursued spiritual studies for nine years in the Himalayas, under the guidance of Swami Sivananda and the tutelage of Swami Tapovanam. He eventually came to share this Vedāntic knowledge with the masses, in the form of the dynamic teacher known as Swami Chinmayananda.

Śrī Gurudev, as he is known to his devotees, is renowned worldwide as a spiritual Master and one of the foremost teachers of *Bhagavad-gītā.* He is credited with the renaissance of spirituality and cultural values in India, and with the spreading of the ageless wisdom of Advaita Vedānta, as expounded by Ādi Śaṅkarācārya, throughout the world.

Swami Chinmayananda attained mahāsamādhi in August 1993. His legacy remains in the form of written, audio, and video publications; social service projects; Vedānta teachers whom he taught and inspired; and Chinmaya Mission centres worldwide, which serve the spiritual and cultural needs of local communities.

Additional biographical information can be found in *Journey of a Master, Ageless Guru, Swami Chinmayananda: A Life of Inspiration and Service, At Every Breath A Teaching,* and *Swami Chinmayananda Reader,* which are available from Chinmaya Publications (ccmtpublications@ chinmayamission.com).

Granny did you have all those lines when you were little like me??

1

GRACEFUL AGEING

From the Graceless to the Graceful

The very fact that we are interested in learning the art of graceful ageing shows that we are already ageing gracefully. Yet we all also know that this process can always be further enhanced and enriched.

Parenting is one of the various facets of graceful ageing. Many parents have raised their children well, perhaps without even knowing the art and science behind it. Doing something good is a good thing, but if we knowingly do something good, it is even better.

When I first thought about the art of graceful ageing, it occurred to me that there must also be an 'art of disgraceful ageing'. But for the latter, no art is required – merely living based on one's impulses, whims and fancies is disgraceful enough.

Then there is 'graceless ageing' – when a man in his old age has nothing to show to people except his age. Life is not just about gold medals or certificates. Sometimes, a person has climbed to the top of the so-called ladder of success, only to find out in his old age that the ladder was on the wrong wall! While he climbs, all the time he feels he is doing wonderfully, for, he sees everyone applauding. But when he reaches the top, he realizes, 'But this is not the place I wanted to reach!'

If life goes on monotonously, and there is no joy or inspiration within, nothing to show for the years, the only thing one can say is, 'I am old.' No one likes to hear the word 'old', which is why many use the term 'senior citizen' instead. No one says, 'Old is gold', anymore. I have met many elderly people, and in general, they usually complain. Only one person told me that old age is the best phase of life. He said, "By then, a person has already seen the world, gone through all the whims and fancies of youth and the mind is much more calm, quiet and understanding."

Once we know what disgraceful way of ageing is, and what graceless ageing is, we can inquire into what is graceful ageing. In this world there is continuous change. It is the changeless law of nature. Time can never be directly perceived, but we are aware of time, for, it is indirectly experienced by us in the form of change. If a change takes place, then we come to realize how much time has passed. If you were to see a baby who always remains a baby, you will never know how much time has passed, how old the baby is. Only through the perception of change do we become aware of time. And if we become intensely aware of time, we will feel a great urgency to question our life. We will realize how quickly time is passing and wonder what we have really accomplished in life.

From Rebirth to No Birth

Changes are taking place everywhere. A tree will grow only as a tree, a creeper will grow only as a creeper, and a flower will grow only as a flower. Trees that grow only in a hot climate will not survive the cold, and vice versa. As compared to plants and trees, animals and birds have more freedom, for, they can move from place to place. But again, as these living creatures are born, so they will remain. For, while changes do take place in these plants and animals, they do not have the ability to consciously make any changes or take decisions such as, 'I am going to do this' or 'I will become that.' This is also why they don't need a seminar on ageing.

We see that at the physical level, or any other level for that matter, even if we do or do not take proper care, we will change regardless. Whether this change is good or bad is a different issue. Here, the most important point is that as human beings we can consciously change; we can consciously bring about our inner and outer transformation. And because we possess

this special faculty, we must utilize it to its optimum, which is why we need every kind of formal or informal education or training, so that we make the best of our lives.

Basically, all of us have committed a big mistake unknowingly – and that big mistake is being born. If we were not born, there would not be any problem at all! We exist, are born, and grow.[1] Once born, the ageing process begins. We cannot say, "I will not grow." We may say this with reference to spirituality, but we cannot stop growing physically. The fundamental problem is that we are born. So, the fundamental solution is to not be born again, which is why spiritual seekers strive for Liberation (mokṣa). Otherwise, 'we are born again and again, and die to be born again in the mother's womb.'[2] And remember, here, 'mother's womb' does not necessarily mean only a human mother, because when the individual (jīva) goes through transmigration, he can enter the womb of any being. In this

1 अस्ति, जायते, वर्धते।

2 पुनरपि जननं पुनरपि मरणं पुनरपि जननीजठरे शयनम्। - भज गोविन्दम्-२१

way, the cycle of life and death just goes on and on, which is why the Lord says, "Those who come to Me, Arjuna, are not born again."[1] He also says that when we know the Truth we attain immortality.[2] To attain freedom from the cycle of birth and death, knowledge of the Self is the only way.

Thus, we must make an effort not to be reborn. No birth, no saṁsāra. Such a beautiful idea – Freedom! No punarjanma. No disgraceful ageing, no graceless ageing, no graceful ageing. No problem at all. Complete

---

1 मामुपेत्य तु कौन्तेय पुनर्जन्म न विद्यते। - भगवद्-गीता-८·१६

2 ...यज्ज्ञात्वामृतमश्नुते। - भगवद्-गीता-१३·१३

freedom. This is what our scriptures lead us to – complete spiritual enlightenment.

An elderly man went to his elderly friend. When he reached there, he found that his friend was not home, only the daughter-in-law. So, he talked with her. During their conversation, he asked, "How old are you?" And because he was an old man, he could ask openly – otherwise, to ask a lady her age is rather difficult. She said, "25 years." "Your husband?" She answered, "My husband is 15 years old." He asked, "What! What about your father-in-law?" She said, "10." The old man became more curious. He asked, "How old is your mother-in-law?" She said, "O! She is just born."

What funny answers! He asked, "Are you saying these things because you are angry with your husband and in-laws?" She said, "Not at all – no! We all have wonderful relationship amongst ourselves. There is no problem at all. We are very happy."

Perplexed he said, "Please explain your answers."

She said, "Actually, my age is 35, but I said 25 because the first ten years were wasted. I never lived consciously nor did I remember God. There was no spirituality in my life at all. Only after I was 10 years, by some Mahātmā's grace, I started living consciously and spiritually. So now I start counting my age only from that day, because that was when I can say I really started living."

The rest of her answers were also clear now – "My husband has been living consciously for the last 15 years, my father-in-law for 10 years. And my mother-in-law has just started, but at least she has started. Better late than never!"

Grace comes only when we start living a beautiful, spiritual life. Otherwise, the days merely come and go. Conscious living, and remembrance of the Lord, is how we make our lives meaningful, joyful, and a blessing to ourselves and others. This is called 'graceful ageing'.

2

THE STAGES OF LIFE

A Lifelong Process

Everything changes in time; it is a natural process. But human beings also have the ability to change consciously. Conscious changes for the better are seen in a lifestyle of graceful ageing. This means not to live merely on impulses. Śrī Ādi Śaṅkarācārya guides us on graceless ageing – during one's childhood, one is attached to toys and play – nothing more. In youth, we spend time pursuing and getting attached to girls and boys. And in old age, there is only worry. Man has hundreds of worries about countless things – wealth, health, neglect, loneliness and much more. Alas, no one is interested in the highest Truth, Brahman.[1]

Being attached to toys in childhood, love-play of youth, and worries in old age, is not

[1] बालस्तावत्क्रीडासक्तः तरुणस्तावत्तरुणीसक्तः ।
वृद्धस्तावच्चिन्तासक्तः परमे ब्रह्मणि कोऽपि न सक्तः ॥ - भज गोविन्दम्-७

called graceful living. It is said, as we age our hair turn grey, or white, or fall down. The teeth start shaking and fall out. But unfortunately our desire for wealth and enjoyment becomes younger and younger.[1] The whole body is worn out, but man's desires for worldly pleasures remain ever young, ever strong, and ever growing. When we receive the wedding invitation of an 80 year old man, how does it make us feel? Forget about 80, even if he is a 60 year old – is this the age to get married? There is no grace in it.

Ādi Śaṅkarācārya also says, "The body is shaking, the head is grey, the mouth has become toothless, and the old man is walking with a stick. There is nothing wrong with these things, because in old age, this is what naturally happens. But the sad part is – he is still full of desires."[2] Some elderly people insist, "I have to go to America!" Arey bhāī, why do you

---

1 जीर्यन्ति जीर्यतः केशा दन्ता जीर्यन्ति जीर्यतः
जीविताशा धनाशा च जीर्यतोऽपि न जीर्यति । – हरिवंश महापुराण-१·३०·४३

2 अंङ्गं गलितं पलितं मुण्डं दशनविहीनं जातं तुण्डम् ।
वृद्धो याति गृहीत्वा दण्डं तदपि न मुञ्चत्याशापिण्डम् ॥ – भज गोविन्दम्-१५

need to go at this age when you cannot even take the flight? There are people who when they become old become renunciates. But if they take sannyāsa only for the sake of getting a free meal for the rest of the life, then even that is not right.

It is important to remember that we cannot start ageing gracefully suddenly in old age – it is a lifelong process. Consider the one who has always lived a licentious life and in old age wants to be self-controlled. Is it possible? Possible but very difficult, except for some rare persons like Ajāmila, who could truly transform in old age. But this is not the norm. Without conscious efforts made early in life, even if one may attend spiritual camps and *Graceful Ageing* seminars, inner transformation does not come about easily. When the yoga instructor said, "Bend down and touch your toes," one old man said, "If God wanted me to touch my toes, he would have given them on my knees!" In old age, there is much less flexibility, at many levels. So, making major changes late in life is quite difficult. Thus, we must start ageing gracefully right from our childhood.

If one remains attached only to toys as a child, only to physical sense pleasures as a youth, and only to worries as an elderly person, what is the use of such a life? Someone may say, "A child is a child – he will be attached to toys!" This is true, but there should also be a conscious effort towards a higher ideal. A verse which was composed by me illustrates how we should live in each stage of life. It means –

'In childhood, one should be attached to śikṣā (education and learning). In youth, one should abide in dīkṣā (vows; firm resolve to serve society with the knowledge gained). In old age, one should live on bhikṣā (contentment with whatever comes in life). Such a person alone can revel in Brahman (Truth)'.[1]

Śikṣā means learning. It also means discipline. Children should play, but they

---

[1] बालस्तावत्शिक्षासक्तः तरुणस्तावत्दीक्षानिष्ठः ।
वृद्धस्तावत्भिक्षावृत्तः स एव ब्रह्मणि सदानुरक्तः ॥

must also be given śikṣā. In youth, yes, there is a strong physical attraction, but one must also take dīkṣā in life. Dīkṣā means a vrata, or vow, and in this verse, it means developing firm resolve and a higher vision, right from a young age. When we retire, enter vānaprastha āśrama, we must learn to be content with whatever comes to us in life (bhikṣā-vṛttaḥ). When we live such a life of calmness and acceptance, we thereafter come to revel in the Truth (Parabrahma).

A Disciplined Childhood

bālastāvat śikṣāsaktaḥ – Let children also be introduced to śikṣā – to learning, studies and discipline. They may be attached to toys, but we can introduce them to culture and spirituality. We can take them to a Bala Vihar class. They should play, but we must also teach them to live a cultured and disciplined life.

One day, I had an interesting dialogue with a nine year old girl. She came to the āśrama with her mother, along with two or three friends.

I asked her, "Do you like to go to school?" She said, "No." I asked, "Do you like to play?"

She said, "Yes, playing is fun. So I asked her, "Now, suppose you only play and do not go to school, will that be fine?" She said, "No."

So she did have some understanding. Even though she likes to play and doesn't like to go to school, she knew that a life of play alone would not be right. At least she knew that education and learning are important.

I further said, "You think that playing is fun, but learning is not fun. That's why you don't like learning, isn't it? But suppose learning becomes fun, a great sport and joy. Then would you like to go to school?" She said, "Then, of course, there is no problem in going to school."

So, what we have to do is make learning a joyous experience. Anybody would dislike school, seeing the whole schooling system, as it is presently. I am afraid of rebirth for this reason – I would have to go to school all over again!

Our Param Guru Swami Tapovanam went to a formal school and later told his father, "I will not go to school anymore. But that does not mean that I will stop learning." His education went on.

Mark Twain said, "I have never let my schooling interfere with my education." This does not mean we should only find fault with formal education, but we should ensure that there is also śikṣā in it. It is the duty of the elders to see that children play as well as learn, so that children are śikṣā-saktaḥ. This was Pūjya Gurudev's main concept behind Chinmaya Vidyalayas and 'Chinmaya Bala Vihar' – Chinmaya Mission's spiritual and value education programme for children.

Values for a Firm Resolve

taruṇastāvat dīkṣā-niṣṭhaḥ – In youth, yes, there is a strong sense of physical attraction between the genders, but that is just one aspect of being young. One should also take dīkṣā in life. Dīkṣā means a vrata, or vow. With proper learning, there will be a resolve from a young age. Because of this, there comes culture and higher aspirations in life. So first śikṣā, then dīkṣā.

Dīkṣā for youth is vital, for, it moulds our thinking and gives a vision in life. Sometimes, students graduate and get a degree, but do not get a job. Often they choose only those careers that pay the highest salaries, instead of choosing professions of their aptitude and talent. The corporate world has the problem of finding 'qualified people' and retaining them. Theirs is a competitive, 'hire and fire' world, and their employees too go wherever the pay is higher. Now imagine how difficult it is for charitable or social organizations to get and retain qualified honorary workers!

One man placed an interesting newspaper advertisement that read, 'All candidates seeking a job may apply. Whatever be your degree, jobs will be given.' Naturally, thousands applied. The man asked each candidate two standard questions. "What is your educational qualification?" and "How much pay do you expect?"

One applicant said, "I have an M.A. in economics and I expect a salary of Rs. 10,000/- to start with." The interviewer said, "Given." The applicant said, "Great! I have never had such a simple interview. Thank you! Now, tell me what do I have to do."

The interviewer in turn asked, "You tell me what you can do with your qualifications to improve the economy of this city?" The applicant seemed confounded and became dumbfounded. He had never thought about it. All he wanted was a fat pay check.

It is hard to find people with a vision. People merely want jobs. But they never have higher vision or think of the bigger picture. Then how can we help improve current situations and solve prevalent problems? This very thinking process is missing! Dīkṣā means having a vision. An economics student who has a higher vision (dīkṣā) will think how the national or global economy can be strengthened. He may have simple plans to begin with, but he can take his plans to higher levels.

The youth who has received dīkṣā will strive to achieve more. When India was under foreign rule, we had young men who had a vision. They went to England, studied and learned how India was being exploited and came back to fight for it's freedom.

So, whether it is in politics, economics, sports, the arts, the sciences, spirituality, or any other field; great achievements have come through dīkṣā alone. Greater good for oneself and others is accomplished through dīkṣā. Such people are not content merely with fulfilling their own needs but strive also for the welfare of all.

Retiring with Grace

vṛddhastāvat bhikṣā-vṛttaḥ – In old age, when we enter vānaprastha āśrama and retire, there must be bhikṣā-vṛttaḥ. The food we get by begging is bhikṣā. The idea here is not to beg for food, but to have total contentment with life as it comes to us[1]. In this stage of life, we should not crave or hanker only for good food, clothing, house and so on. Everything should be accepted as it is, without complaint. A bhikṣu and a beggar are different. When a bhikṣu begs for alms, he is not called a beggar, for, he merely fulfils his basic needs, living contentedly with whatever comes to him. Brahmacārīs and sannyāsīs who go to different houses for bhikṣā cannot say, 'Give me laḍḍū and peḍā because today is my birthday.' They should accept whatever is given.

When we have worked hard all our life for food, clothing and shelter, we should thereafter fully dedicate ourself to spirituality. We may have had a spiritual inclination, but this is the time when spirituality alone should be our goal. It is the time to be completely content with whatever life offers.

---

1 यदृच्छालाभसन्तुष्टः... - भगवद्-गीता-४·२२

The literal meaning of vānaprastha is 'one who lives in the forest'. It also means living in a solitary place away from family and children. (Vanam – forest / away from home + stha – staying = vānaprastha). Vānaprastha indicates a life of solitude. In our times staying in the vanam means residing alone or independently, withdrawn from social activities. In the word 'vānaprastha', 'pra' indicates completely or totally. This means to be completely away from constant phone calls and e-mails checking up on everyone, finding out how they are, or hearing the latest gossip. Some say, "I am in vānaprastha āśrama. My son's flat is above mine." This is not really a solitary place, but for many, even this much is fine.

In the Upaniṣads, a different meaning is given for the word 'vanam'. Here, Paramātmā (the supreme Self or supreme Lord who is most adorable and worshipful), is called vanam[1]. Thus, the meaning of vānaprastha is also 'one who intends to abide in the Self / Brahman alone.'

Brahmacārī (student) means 'one who revels or wants to revel in Brahman, whose

1 तद्ध तद्वनं नाम तद्वनमित्युपासितव्यं... - केनोपनिषद्-४·६

very nature is Brahman.'[1] Brahman means the supreme Self, but the word also refers to the Vedas. So, in the beginning, the student must study and be devoted to the Vedas. But the Vedas should be studied only for knowing Brahman. Later, when one enters vānaprastha, the goal should be to revel in Brahma, the Self of all beings. One who thus meditates on the worshipful Brahman as 'tadvanam' then all beings including trees, plants, birds, animals and of course humans, love him.[2] For, it cannot be possible that one who is spiritually unfolding, is not loved by all. All love to be in his or her company.

1 ब्रह्माणि चरति इति ।

2 ...सर्वाणि भूतानि संवाञ्छन्ति ॥ - केनोपनिषद्-४.६

We may have experienced this feeling that everyone is ignoring us. But a true vānaprastha, is welcomed everywhere because he loves all as his own Self. This is graceful ageing.

The Point of No Return

sa eva brahmaṇi sadānuraktaḥ – The bhikṣā-vṛtta vānaprastha revels in Brahman alone. This is basically the goal of, and connecting threads between, all the four stages of life (āśramas) – student (brahmacarya), householder (gṛhastha), retired (vānaprastha), and renunciate (sannyāsa). I read an interesting statement about the four āśramas – In brahmacarya āśrama, you 'learn', in gṛhastha āśrama, you 'earn', in vānaprastha āśrama, you 'turn', and from sannyāsa, there is 'no return'.

In gṛhastha āśrama, when we say earn, it does not mean only money. As a gṛhastha, we should earn wealth for ourselves and the society. We can also earn name, fame, power and much more. But in vānaprastha, we must turn towards God/Self. Pūjya Gurudev Swami

Chinmayananda would say, "Take a U-turn." Sant Kabīra says, "Turn towards that land of immortality from whence we have come."[1] Paramātmā is our true origin. That is where you have to go back. So turn now towards Him.

After turning towards God in vānaprastha āśrama, then in sannyāsa, there is no return! For example, the river Ganga, flows from Gomukh to the Bay of Bengal. It returns to the ocean – its origin. Vānaprastha is like this turning towards the source, which culminates in sannyāsa. If we revel in learning, have discipline and resolve, and are content with whatever we get in life, then, such a person alone ages gracefully and comes to revel in the supreme Truth (Brahman).

1 अमर वह देशवा जहाँ से आयो ॥... - संत कबीर

3

ŚIKṢĀ

Passing the Torch

As students everyone must be given śikṣā. The first chapter of *Taittirīya-upaniṣad* is called 'Śīkṣā vallī'. It concluded with the graduation address that the Guru gives the students before they leave the gurukula. These are the final instructions they receive from their teacher. Throughout their stay of 10-12 years, they would have learned various subjects and received many types of detailed instructions. But finally the Guru gives some guiding principles on how to lead a good life. So much is taught over the years, but what is the essence of all these teachings? What are the basic, fundamental principles to be remembered at all times?

People would buy books – for instance, the *Bhagavad-gītā* with commentary – and then request, Pūjya Gurudev, "Please autograph this and write a message for me." Now, the whole book is a message, isn't it? But they would think of it as an extensively long message, so they would ask for a short and personal message meant just for them. So Pūjya Gurudev would sign and write "Read this book 15 times," or he would write, "Read two pages every day," like a doctor's prescription. I found that very few people followed these instructions, even though they asked for a personal message or specific guidance.

In newspaper, magazine, TV or radio interviews, usually in the end they ask, "What is your message for our readers or listeners or viewers?" In the same way, in his valedictory address, the Guru says, "I have taught you many things, but I want to tell you some salient points that you must keep in mind. No matter what your profession, these are some important aspects that are common guidelines for all."

vedam-anūcyācārya-antevāsinam-anuśāsti – Having taught all the Vedas, the Ācārya/ Guru gives his final instructions and guiding principles for students to remember and adhere to as they live and work.

When Lord Rāma wanted to give one last chance to Rāvaṇa to surrender before the war, he asked Aṅgada to go as a messenger. Aṅgada asked, "Bhagavān, I will go there, but please give me some guidelines. Keeping those in mind, I will act accordingly and speak to Rāvaṇa." Bhagavān said to Aṅgada, "Our mission has to be accomplished and yet, no harm must come to Rāvaṇa.[1] Remembering this you may say or do all that needs to be done. In this lies our welfare as well as that of Rāvaṇa. Keep this in mind and go."

Similarly, the Guru also states the common, fundamental guidelines that all should follow, regardless of profession, social status, gender, religion and so on.

May Truth Be Told

satyaṁ vada – Speak the truth. In another mantra in the same Upaniṣad, it is again said, Don't be careless in speaking the truth.[2]

1 काजु हमार तासु हित होई। - श्रीरामचरितमानस-६·१६·४

2 सत्यान्न प्रमदितव्यम्। - तैत्तिरीय-उपनिषद्-१·११·१

If someone asks us, "Can you do this job?", then we should speak the truth. There are some people who are wonderful at taking on tasks and doing nothing about them. If we can't do something or don't want to, we should say so truthfully, so that the other person doesn't depend on us. But if we make a promise, we should fulfil it (satyaṁ vada). If we are asked about someone, and we do not know anything about him or her, we should not give any opinion. It is not our business to stamp someone as a good or bad person. Clearly and definitely say, "I don't know."

But why should I speak the truth? Let us say some person ask me my name. To one person I say, "Swami Ghanananda." To another I say, "Swami Gananananda." To the third I say, "Swami Nandananda." Now I will have to remember to which person I have told which name. Imagine the confusion! Naturally, one day, the lies will be uncovered and my bluff will be called. By not living a life of truthfulness, I create problems for myself and suffer.

By not speaking the truth, one slowly creates a split personality in oneself, but the biggest loss is the loss of one's credibility. There is a famous story of a shepherd who would needlessly cry out, "Tiger!" When people would come running to help him, he would laugh, "Look how I fooled you!" One day, when the tiger really came, and he cried out for help, no one came to help him, because he had already lost his credibility. When we speak one lie, ten lies follow.

Hold High the Flag of Dharma

dharmaṁ cara – Live a life of dharma, or righteousness. Note that it is not said, 'dharmaṁ vada' (speak dharma). One should not merely speak of ethics, morality and righteousness; but one must live such a life. There are the Ten Commandments in the *Bible* – the dos and don'ts. Sometimes people ask if there are any such commandments in Hindu dharma. Of course there are. Some are spoken of in the following passages.

Dharma is that which integrates our inner personality, our family, our community, and our nation. Satya is very important in maintaining dharma. Speaking the truth is good, but whether it is beneficial, does good (hitaṁ) to the listener or not is more important. Sometimes there is no need of speaking even the truth, when it may be hurtful or could unnecessarily create problems.

If satyam is in keeping with dharma, then we should stick to the truth. But sometimes, for the sake of upholding dharma, we may have to speak an untruth, then know that this is also satyam. For example, a villainous man with evil motives is chasing a woman, and she comes to hide in your house. At that time, if the man comes and asks where she went, you should not say, "Come in! She is in my house." If you speak the truth in this case, it would not be in accordance with dharma, because dharma

is 'that which protects'. By telling an untruth, if you can protect her, then you should. By doing so, you will also protect the man – at least this time – from committing a sinful act.

In *Vālmīki Rāmāyaṇa,* it is said when Śrī Rāma was leaving Ayodhyā in Sumantra's chariot, everyone was crying and following him. At that time, Lord Śrī Rāma told Sumantra, "Move fast," but King Daśaratha came out running after them and said, "Sumantra, stop!" Now what should Sumantra do? The king says, "Stop," and Śrī Rāma, the prince says, "Keep moving." Sumantra was in a dilemma. Śrī Rāma said, "Keep moving. If he questions you later, you tell him there was so much noise that you did not hear him."

So, was Bhagavān encouraging untruth? No, what Bhagavān said was right, because King Daśaratha was emotionally overwhelmed, and therefore, he was trying to prevent his son from leaving. In fact, if he had done so, it would not have been in keeping with dharma.

It was to uphold of dharma that Śrī Rāma was leaving in the first place! Once it was settled that he had to go to the forest, why should he delay his departure. When we get carried away by emotions and sentiments, dharma is lost, and this should not happen at any cost.

Śrī Rāma was the embodiment of dharma. To uphold dharma at all times is very difficult. So his life was very difficult. Who indeed can understand a life of such perfection? Even his enemies knew that Śrī Rāma was the embodiment of dharma.'

I read a beautiful quotation – 'If you don't stand for something, you fall for everything.' Lord Rāma stood for dharma alone and was willing to sacrifice everything for its sake. Whatever we do to uphold dharma is called satyam. For example, while driving in India, we are told to keep in the left lane. We are law-abiding, so we follow rules. But suppose a truck is heading straight in our direction in the left lane. Now, if we say, "I am a law-abiding citizen, and even if the truck is heading towards me, I will not go to the right side," people will surely get the news of your departure from this world! So, while keeping to the left is for everyone's safety, if following that rule puts our life into danger in a particular instance, our first duty is to protect ourself. This is the difference between the letter of the law and the spirit of the law. The spirit is called dharma.

Alert Living

svādhyāyān-mā pramadaḥ – Let there be no inadvertence or negligence in svādhyāya, or self-study. In order to understand truth and dharma we should study the scriptures. Ādi

Śaṅkarācārya says, "Study the Vedas daily."[1] The understanding of dharma is indeed difficult. That is why we must remain steadfast in scriptural studies.

Svādhyāya has many meanings. Doing japa (repetition of mantra) or pārāyaṇa (reading the scripture), or chanting Viṣṇusahasranāma, is also called svādhyāya. Studying two to three pages of a scriptural text everyday is also called svādhyāya. Most importantly, 'svādhyāya' also means, study of oneself or introspection. This study should be done daily, so that we are constantly reminded of the teachings and never lose sight of our ultimate goal.

ācāryāya priyaṁ dhanam-āhṛtya – After learning from the Guru, it is the student's duty to give dakṣiṇā. In earlier days, no fees were collected. The students stayed in the gurukula. Whether one was a prince or a Brāhmaṇa, everyone studied together. At the end of the study, they offered dakṣiṇā as per their capacity. The Guru instructs the students to give what

1 वेदो नित्यमधीयतां... - साधना पञ्चकम्-१

is dear (priyam) to the Guru as dakṣiṇā. It represents the student's heartfelt gratitude to the Guru. This means, from whomsoever we learn something - whether rituals, spiritual knowledge, worship, or secular knowledge, we should always be grateful to that person. In this way, we also respect the Guru-śiṣya tradition.

prajā-tantuṁ mā-vyavacchetsīḥ – Do not break the family lineage. After graduation, and being capable of supporting a family we are instructed to get married, have children, and continue our lineage (vaṁśa paramparā). Whatever culture and values we learn in the gurukula must be passed on to the next generation. Some rare students do not get married and take to the spiritual path full time. They do not have to carry forward the family lineage in terms of children but they continue the Guru-śiṣya paramparā (teacher-taught lineage).

Now, although the Guru has given instructions, he again emphasizes certain points, warns the students never to be negligent or take these teachings lightly.

So, though it was said, 'Speak the truth and follow dharma', he again emphasizes, "Never ever be negligent towards truth or dharma."[1]

kuśalān-na pramaditavyam – Never be negligent towards your welfare. The expression, 'Take care of yourself,' is common. When someone is unwell, we say, "Take care of yourself." To a traveller, we say, "Be careful," meaning, no one else will take care of us. And even if someone is willing to take care of us, we must learn to accept it. We may be unwell,

[1] सत्यान्न प्रमदितव्यम्। धर्मान्न प्रमदितव्यम्। - तैत्तिरीय-उपनिषद्-१·११·१

and our assistant may give us our medications, but we must also be ready to take them. For example, when we travel, our ticket, our bag, our clothes, our passport, our money – all that we need must be with us. Who else will take care of these? And then, of course, there are some other things to be taken care of in life like filing our income tax forms!

bhūtyai na pramaditavyam – Here 'bhūti' means 'prosperity'. Never be negligent towards prosperity. We should earn enough to sustain ourself and our family. For earning more we may need promotions for which we may have to upgrade our professional knowledge. This is called 'bhūti'. When a doctor decides to specialize in a field, it is for bhūti. Hence, we should continue learning throughout our life and be successful in whatever we do.

svādhyāya-pravacanābhyāṁ na pramaditavyam – Do not be negligent in self-study and giving discourses (spreading this knowledge). We should study regularly and keep sharing what we learn. After the study course that we take in Chinmaya Mission, we should become teachers and impart what we have learnt. In this way, our knowledge will be ever relevant

and others too will benefit. It does not mean that we have to make a show of becoming some great Guru. It means we should share our knowledge.

I do not have a disciple named Jagat, so I cannot say I am the Guru of the world! But the world is my Guru.[1] So anyone who thinks that the whole world is my Guru is also called Jagat Guru.

1 जगत् गुरुः यस्य सः जगद्गुरुः ।

Parents should be particularly aware of what their children are learning in their younger years. Often parents want their children to learn Sanskrit prayers, but they themselves don't want to study anything. So when the children end up knowing more than the parents, and when they keep asking questions to which their parents don't have answers, the children start losing respect for their parents. Parents are role models for the children, therefore, their own studies are important for the nurturing of their children.

deva-pitṛ-kāryābhyāṁ na pramaditavyam – One must be steadfast in all duties related to the devatās (deities) and pitṛs (forefathers), without any inadvertence, forgetfulness and

negligence. In Hindu dharma, there are rituals like deva-yajña and pitṛ-yajña.

Here, the term devatās refers to the presiding deities of the forces of nature and the natural elements. We must respect nature and help to maintain ecological balance and live in harmony with nature. We plant trees and celebrate Earth Day, yet we pollute the waters and exploit the earth. The yajña spirit is to value and respect all of nature and not just perform ritualistic fire worship (yajña).

Also we must respect our forefathers who have passed down our traditions, cultures and values. Disrespecting our ancestors, thinking that they knew nothing, and that they were foolish in their beliefs, would make us even greater fools – as according to the law of heredity we would inherit their foolishness. If our fathers knew nothing and their grandfather also knew nothing, then neither do we! All our knowledge comes from others and from the past.

As a world citizen, it is important to give due reverence to our heritage and also global environment.

mātṛ-devo bhava, pitṛ-devo bhava, ācārya-devo bhava, atithi-devo bhava – Consider your mother, father, teacher and guest as God. An atithi is a guest who arrives at your doorstep without an invitation or appointment (a-tithi). These instructions of the Guru are very important. Everything that he has said emphasizes that we should see God/Self everywhere and in everything. We think that God is not seen by us. We should first start

seeing God in those directly present in front of us in the form of our mother, father, Guru and guests. Then we can start recognizing Him elsewhere.

As you sow, so you reap. When we begin to treat our mother, father, Guru and guests as Divine, we can eventually expand this vision to everyone. In this way, we also set a good example for our children and future generations. But if we don't show reverence to anyone, how can we get respect from anyone?

I read a story where a family kept the grandfather in the outhouse. They gave him a bell, so that whenever he needed them, he could ring it. They did not want him to come into the main house. One day, his grandchild took away the bell. When the bell did not ring even once throughout the day, the father began to wonder what had happened. So he went to check on the grandfather, from whom he learned that his son had taken away the bell.

The father called his son, "Why have you taken it away? Where is that bell?" The son said, "I have kept it safely. When you become old, I will give it to you. Then you can ring and call me."

Manu Smṛti says, 'Never insult your mother and father, even in your dream!' They have taken so much pains to bring us into this world and raise us.

The *Taittirīya-upaniṣad* says that we must treat our mother, father, Guru, and guest as God. Remember that at some point, we will also become parents, and become someone's atithi (guest). We must, always protect dharma and do the right thing. For, when dharma is protected, it will protect us, save us, make us prosperous, and even take us to Liberation. It is rightly said that dharma protects those who protect dharma or follow dharma.[1]

Some people complain, "No one follows righteous ways or has values, so why should I?" Can we live an unrighteous life? If we do, then we should be ready to pay the price when the time comes! It is interesting to note that values themselves have never lost their relevance in society. From time immemorial, until today, everyone respects values.The only problem is that now most people respect values in others, but don't strive to live them. We want and expect to see others live a life of values and virtues. We may be corrupt ourselves, but we respect loyalty in others. Even the criminal wants his accountant to be honest, reliable and loyal!

yānyanavadyāni karmāṇi, tāni sevitavyāni, no itarāṇi, yānyasmākaṁsucaritāni, tāni tvayopāsyāni – Follow only good conduct

---

[1] धर्मो रक्षति रक्षितः। - मनु स्मृति-८.१५

and perform only good actions. The Guru acknowledges that we are humans, so we may at times act or think improperly, but we should be careful and alert enough to keep correcting ourselves. Many people think that they are above all laws, rules and regulations, or are perfect and free from faults. But the Guru does not say this. In fact, he even goes so far as to advise the students to follow only the blemish-free actions and thoughts of our Gurus and none others.

In life, there are always different situations and circumstances. Often we are unable to determine our duties, proper conduct or right response towards a particular person or in a given situation. Doubts keep rising in our minds. If we are confused or unable to find the right answer, then the instruction given by the Guru is to approach a good, noble, wise person and follow the advice given, for, such people do not have ulterior motives. Thus, whatever such noble persons do, say, or advise, it should be followed. If we are able to find a solution by ourself, it is good, but if not, we should not let pride get in the way of asking for help.

If we have any doubt about our duty or conduct, we should approach a noble, and wise person, and ask him. Arjuna got confused, in the battlefield, even as the Mahābhārata war was about to commence. He asked the Lord for help.[1]

1 ...शिष्यस्तेऽहं शाधि मां त्वां प्रपन्नम्। - भगवद्-गीता-२·७

4

DĪKṢĀ

Aspire to Inspire

When the child grows up to become a young man, he may or may not get married; he may even become a sannyāsī. Regardless of that, in his youth, it is the duty of his parents and guardians to give him dīkṣā. Dīkṣā initiates one into a life of vratas or 'vows', so that one develops firm resolve in facing life with strength, love and righteousness.

Everyone should have some great aspirations in life - not only that which relates to our profession. We should strive for excellence, in every field - secular or sacred. We should all strive to make this world a better place. At the very least, we should not harm, destroy or worsen it.

To leave the world a better place than when we found it, is a good resolve (vratam).

The *Taittirīya-upaniṣad* teaches us some very important vratas that are worth taking in our life.

Vows of Love and Service

annaṁ na nindyāt, tad-vratam – Do not criticize food. This is the vow. Even though the literal meaning of annaṁ is food, it refers to anything that we enjoy or experience through our sense organs. When it comes to food, its enjoyment begins with our nose – an aroma from the kitchen. So first we smell it and then we see it. Even seeing food that is creatively presented and well-cooked – makes us happy. Then we touch it. "Aah! This idli is so soft, so perfectly steamed!" And then we put it in the mouth, to experience its delicious taste. And finally, we chew our food, and hear the various sounds resulting from the different textures of different foods – some crunchy, some sticky. So, all the five sense organs come into play.

Annaṁ thus refers to the entire world of sense objects. We should not insult, condemn or criticize anything of the world, for, we all need things for sustenance throughout our lives. When a man gets angry, he bangs doors and windows. Do the doors and windows deserve such treatment? They have not done any harm to him. Another person bangs down the phone irritated by a wrong number. But what is the use of breaking the instrument?

We must learn to treat the whole world, even the inert objects with respect. Each object has its own value, its own place in life. All objects may not be equally important, but each object has some importance, some value. Also we should not give undue importance or neglect some object, being or situation. For example, some people say, "I don't care for money!" Don't say so, because money has its own value in life and teaches its own lessons. At the same time, we should not think that money alone matters or money is God.

Never insult or criticize the world. In the larger vision, the whole world is created by the Lord. If we insult the world, we are insulting the Lord. If our mother or wife has cooked food and we throw it out, we are not only insulting the food, but also the one who made it. Therefore, do not insult food. Scriptures teach us the importance of developing 'dispassion'. This is achieved by criticizing our excessive attachments to objects and beings and not the objects themselves. All of us especially the youth must learn and fulfil this vow – never to criticize.

annaṁ na paricakṣīta, tad-vratam – Do not waste food. In the world, everyday, how much food is needlessly thrown away! In some places people are dying of starvation, and in other places they are dying because of overeating. And, in yet other places food is simply being thrown away. In some homes, after eating from a plate, they pour water into the plate, and drink it so that not a single grain of food is wasted.

Many countries speak highly of their progress, yet in such matters, they continue to create grave imbalances by wasting or throwing away all surpluses. For example, the buffet food service. The idea is to let people take as much as they want so that there will not be any wastage. But this is far from what happens. It is seen that people pile their plates as though they have never seen food before and as though they are never going to eat again! They try everything on the menu. So whenever and wherever possible, we should only take as much as we need.

Similarly, so many other things also continue to be wasted. Disposable items that don't disintegrate create so many problems. Where can so much garbage be thrown? In the past, after the eldest child in the family played with a toy, the second and third child would play with the same toy. Now each child has so many toys! What will they do with all of them? In earlier days, a cloth bag was used for years to buy groceries from the market, and it was washed and reused. Then it became fashionable to use plastic bags. Now, they are again advocating use of the cloth bag. We are finally coming to understand that by small changes, large problems can be created or solved. Once we get used to comforts, if we have to go back to basics, it becomes very difficult. The results of wasting or not wasting, are far-reaching.

annaṁ bahu kurvīta, tad-vratam – Grow more food! There should not be any scarcity. There should be plenty. Today, agricultural lands are being converted into non-agricultural lands for building construction. Cultivatable land is disappearing. Where will we cultivate crops and vegetables if this goes on? Man is no more living in harmony with nature. In the past, agriculture was considered a very good occupation, but now the best jobs are in IT, although, the fundamental need is food. We cannot live without food. Without iPhones and computers we can probably live more happily. Food is the first necessity. Countries that continue to grow their own food and enrich their food sources will naturally have more power in the world.

If we reflect deeply on all these vows, we will gain a totally different vision, one that is more holistic. Some people say that Hindu dharma propounds an escapist or otherworldly philosophy, but that is not true! The scriptures do not say one should not have material prosperity. During India's Golden Age, under the reign of the Maurya dynasty, there was immense prosperity and progress in all fields. But today, prosperity comes at an incredibly high cost. Excessive pollution, global warming with air and water contamination, and natural disasters are the results. Man is greatly affected physically, spiritually and culturally. We must enrich ourselves – materially, culturally, socially and spiritually. That is the meaning of 'Grow more food'.

na kañcana vasatau pratyācakṣīta, tad-vratam – When anyone comes to our house, do not turn him away. It is already said treat the guest as God.[1] All that we possess is meant for serving the world. Therefore, we must take a vow that, 'May I never insult what I get, not waste what I have, I must produce more, enrich myself and become prosperous', not just for my own enjoyment, but for sharing it with everyone.

tasmād-yayā kayā ca vidhayā bahu-annaṁ prāpnuyāt – Therefore, we must always have plenty of everything in our homes. These

---

[1] अतिथि देवो भव ।

instructions are not for renunciates, but for householders and for youngsters who will become householders. We must have plenty so that we can offer it to anyone who comes to us. When a guest visits our home, for however short or long a time, we must give him food and a place to stay. Don't send him to a restaurant. In fact, we should not ask, "Will you eat?" but offer food without asking or being asked.

ārādhyasmā annam-ityācakṣate – The Upaniṣads instruct that we should say, "Sir, food is ready." Do not ask, "What will you have?" because what if he asks for something that you don't have? So the best thing is to just give what we have. And ensure that we always have plenty, not only for our own needs and comforts but also for serving others.

etad-vai mukhato'nnaṁ-rāddham – We receive food and all other things in life depending on the manner in which we give these to others. If we offer things with love and respect, then we too will receive in the same manner. If we offer with honour then we also will receive it in the same manner. And if we give insultingly or disrespectfully, then we also will get all things in the same manner. In this world we see that some people do get things, but always with insults. Why? There must be a reason – there cannot be an effect without a cause. Some always get the royal treatment everywhere they go. There are many examples in history where guests were welcomed and served with love and respect, even if the hosts did not have enough for themselves. As a result of their observance of such values, they always earned great blessings. All these vratas are applicable to householders. When they follow them, their lives will be graceful.

An Altar-ed Life

Dīkṣā will guide the youth in all aspects of life. For example, when someone devotes his life to music, not only will music make him famous, but his accomplishments will also enrich the field of music. Each help the other, so it is hard to tell whether the art has made the artist great or the artist has made the art greater.

There are many dangers in living a life without a vision and higher purpose. I remember seeing a poster in a youngster's room – 'Don't drink and drive. Smoke and fly.' Unfortunately, many really do smoke or drink their lives away! Graduating medical students are asked to take an oath that they will use their knowledge for serving society. But often, because they have to repay large student loans or get back the capitation fees they have given, they focus only on becoming debt-free and rich. A vicious cycle of exploitation begins.

The doctor wants to take as much money from the patient. The patient in turn as a businessman takes as much money as possible from the doctor, when he comes to him as a customer.

One of the highest teachings of dīkṣā is dedicating to God everything that one does, in whatever field we work. By all that we do with our body, mind and speech we offer as a worship of God. Through this attitude we grow stronger. There are many talented and accomplished people who do not have a high altar of dedication in their life. Their altar is solely their own pleasure. But how much fulfillment can this give?

I read a beautiful line – 'An altar in life alters your life.' The higher the altar, the greater the transformation. Dedication to an altar – whether God, your parents, your teachers, or society at large – inspires and transforms. When the altar of dedication is low, we do not unfold within. In the lives of extraordinary men, we see that they always have an altar of dedication and that makes their life distinguished. Without an altar of dedication our life is ordinary, may be it is good, but it is nothing special. People become great and their life graceful and beautiful only when they work with dedication for a higher cause.

The altar of dedication is the key in dīkṣā. Śrī Kṛṣṇa has said, "Whatever we do, enjoy, sacrifice or give, offer it to the Lord."[1]

[1] यत्करोषि यदश्नासि यज्जुहोषि ददासि यत्।
यत्तपस्यसि कौन्तेय तत्कुरुष्व मदर्पणम्॥ – भगवद्-गीता-९.२७

Even when we give a few coins to a roadside beggar, do not think that we are giving them to a beggar. Think that we are giving them to the Lord. Living such a life is graceful living.

There is a famous story. King Akbara asked Tānsena, "You sing well, but your teacher, Śrī Haridāsa Mahārāja is greater. His singing is divine. Why is it so. Tānsena replied, "Because he sings for God and I sing to please you!"

When we do all our actions as worship of the Lord, we can attain perfection.[1] We need not do any specific, or special actions. Whatever we are capable of doing, whichever is our enjoined duty, whatever test we are given, we should do it as our worship of the Lord. This becomes a great blessing.

1 स्वकर्मणा तमभ्यर्च्य सिद्धिं विन्दति मानवः। - भगवद्-गीता-१८.४६

5

THE VAIRĀGYA OF VĀNAPRASTHA

Embrace Sādhanā

When we read the instructions given for vānaprastha āśrama (retired age), we may get frightened – because the two most important practices given are tapas and īkṣa. Tapas means 'penance' or 'austerity'. Īkṣa means 'seeing the Self'. In the summertime, the vānaprastha is told to do Pañcāgni tapas, for which all the mahārājās of yore would leave their kingdoms and retire to the forest.

King Pṛthu went to the forest to perform Pañcāgni tapas (five fire austerity). He sat in the open grounds, from sunrise to sunset, with fire burning on all four sides of him, and the sun was the fifth 'fire' above him. In the rainy season, he sat bare body under the lashing rain. In the winter, he stood in the icy river, with water up to his throat.

Isn't it frightening? We can barely stand a lukewarm shower much less put one toe into icy waters!

Don't worry, there is hope for us. In *Tulasī Rāmāyaṇa,* Bhagavān Rāma describes nine kinds of devotion to Śabarī. The Lord says, "The sixth kind of devotion is to consistently practise more sense control, withdrawing from excessive worldly activities, and engaging only in those practices which saintly people follow."[1]

1 छठ दम सील बिरति बहु करमा । निरत निरंतर सज्जन धरमा ॥
– श्रीरामचरितमानस–३·३५·१

When one is a student, his time should be devoted to learning and to the service of the Guru, according to the gurukula tradition. One must study first. Then, as he enters a life of greater activity, he will have to allocate most of his time to all his duties – family, professional, social and so on. With so many duties and responsibilities, one's personal spiritual practices (sādhanā) is limited to a little time spent in japa, meditation or pūjā. But whatever we do, it can be done with the attitude of worship to God. This makes life 100% spiritual.

When we retire vānaprastha āśrama, spiritual practices should take up 75% of our time. Householders always complain, "I never get time to do any kind of sādhanā. The telephone starts ringing whenever I sit for meditation." After retirement we can really hook off from everything. Our time should be primarily spent in sādhanā. We can keep some time for meeting people when necessary, to help others in need, or to advise our children if they ask for it. Nothing more than that. We should not keep calling our children everyday to ask how they are and what they are doing. Let them live their lives as they like. We should

not feel bad if our son buys a sofa set without consulting us!

We should not go anywhere needlessly. Attend satsaṅga or pūjās. Do not say yes to invitation for every social event. Some elderly people spend all their time playing cards, watching TV, or partying. Countless elderly people spend long hours and lot of money to look younger through makeup, face lifts, plastic surgery and what not. We may be able to trick some people into thinking we are younger than our real age, but we cannot trick a flight of stairs! We can live a less wasteful and more productive life. Earlier we complained about never having enough time for spiritual practices, so now, when the time is available, we must be wise and keep ourselves engaged in spiritual practices. This is graceful ageing.

Long for God

Tulasīdāsa writes that man should feel sad that his life has passed by without knowing God. He should ask, "When will I love God, develop dispassion for the world and get a saintly mind?" The interesting point is that this is possible only by God's grace! Therefore, we must invoke God's grace through sincere prayer.

Tulasīdāsa prays for a saintly nature without any craving, filled with contentment, and resolute in thought, word and deed. He asks for a life that is always engaged in serving others. He says, "Even if I hear harsh or hurtful words, let me not burn in that fire. Let my mind be calm." He prays that he be free from ego, free from gossip and idle talk of the virtues and vices of others and to give up all worries originating from body-identification. Knowing that all sorrows steal one's equanimity, he prays, 'May I get unswerving devotion for the lotus feet of the Lord!'

When we are firmly convinced that we must get established in the Truth we will live life accordingly to achieve this goal. A man who has such a noble goal naturally ages gracefully.

6

THE BLISS OF SANNYĀSA

Blessed Indeed

Living a graceful life does not happen in a few days, weeks or months. It is a long process, but if followed, its rewards are great indeed. In childhood, there is śikṣā with saṁskāra-yukta anuśāsanam (learning discipline with values). In youth and adulthood, there is dīkṣā with vicāra-yukta ācaraṇam (living with right thinking). And in old age, there is vairāgya-yukta śāstra-adhyayanam (living with dispassion and scriptural study). Then we come to life's most beautiful stage, its culmination, sannyāsa (renouncing the world and revelling in the Self).

Since student life focuses on studies, and adult life on fulfilling various responsibilities, people feel they have less time to practise spiritual disciplines. In vānaprastha āśrama,

75% of one's time is to be devoted to sādhanā and 25% to worldly interactions. But in sannyāsa, 100% of one's time should be only for spiritual practices.

Ādi Śaṅkarācārya says about sannyāsa, "Ever revelling in the teachings of Vedānta, and ever content with a beggar's morsel, full of compassion they roam about free from sorrow. Blessed indeed are these sannyāsīs, though they wear (only) a loincloth."[1]

Ādi Śaṅkara says that the most fortunate and blessed are indeed those who have fulfilled their life and thus, they are able to live contentedly with as little as possible (just a loincloth to cover themselves). Ādi Śaṅkara is not referring to an ordinary person who is poor, homeless, or the tribals living in forests. Kaupīnavantaḥ refers to sannyāsīs or 'renunciates'. The loin-cloth symbolizes total dispassion. Indeed, such sannyāsīs are

---

[1] वेदान्तवाक्येषु सदा रमन्तो भिक्षान्नमात्रेण च तुष्टिमन्तः ।
विशोकवन्तः करुणैकवन्तः कौपीनवन्तः खलु भाग्यवन्तः ॥
- कौपीन पञ्चकम्-१

the most fortunate, for, their cloth represents their fulfilment of, and contentment with, life in its entirety. Therefore, as far as worldly life is concerned, the sannyāsī's needs are basic, and with whatever little he gets – food, shelter or clothing, he is satisfied. Nothing more is needed.

Many people, especially the younger generation, pity sannyāsīs. On one hand, they admire and prostrate to Swamis, but within they feel, 'Aah! Poor thing!' Sometimes people ask, "Swamiji, do you have any regrets about taking sannyāsa?" When I was in the ninth standard in school, there was a sannyāsī from Haridwar who used to come to our town. He was a tall, bright, brilliant monk – even now I can clearly visualize him. As I went to school, I would see him on his morning walk, and I would think, 'What kind of a life he must be living! It must be so boring. He doesn't go to movies or restaurants – and so he must not be having any fun!' Now I am a sannyāsī and know that it is joyful.

Even though he has completely renounced worldly life and has no possessions whatsoever, he is most fortunate (bhāgyavantaḥ). That is why people call a renunciate 'Mahārāja' (a great king). Such a person ever revels in the Upaniṣadic declarations, and is transported into great heights with its meaning and depth. I am the illuminator; I am everything and I am beyond everything. This is the truth described in the Upaniṣads. To know this joy, we have to experience it. When people see a Realized Master, they do not understand him. It is something like when we are listening to music (with earphones), but the other person cannot hear any sound. We are revelling, but the other person is just watching, for, we are experiencing something he does not know.

Compassion Embodied

The spiritual Master, is totally free from grief; he has no sorrows at all. Yet, he is exceedingly compassionate to others' sorrows. Someone who wears the clothes of a sannyāsī, but still remains unhappy all the time, has not understood the glory of sannyāsa and the knowledge of the Truth. For, in fact, sannyāsa is a state of complete and total Bliss.

The sannyāsī has understood that the whole world is an appearance, and that the Truth alone is real. When he sees suffering, he knows that it is simply due to one's own wrong thinking and wrong notions. But when they see others suffering, they do not say, "Your sorrow is an illusion." They are compassionate, and they advise each person at their own level, and help them to come out of their sorrow and lift their attention to the higher Truth.

At the time of sannyāsa dīkṣā (initiation ceremony into sannyāsa), the Guru gives a sannyāsa mantra. The initiated sannyāsī contemplates on that mantra or on any form (saguṇa-rūpa) of the Lord. He chants, 'Om Namaḥ Śivāya', or any other mantra, and meditates on the Lord in his heart. Whether revelling in the form or formless Truth, he is always in the highest state. Ādi Śaṅkarācārya says that such spiritual Masters roam in this world like the spring season. Just as spring makes the flowers blossom, so too, such sannyāsīs bring about joy, sanctify and bring about an inner blossoming in all spiritual seekers. Such sannyāsīs are indeed blessed and so are others who come in contact with them.

The Gift of Fearlessness

The culmination of all sādhanā is in revelling in God with devotion. And what will such a person, who revels in Paramātmā, give to this world? We can only give what we have. He is in bliss, so he gives bliss. He has knowledge, so he gives knowledge. Indeed, the greatest gift that a true sannyāsī bestows upon all those around him is the gift of fearlessness. If I own something and see that someone else wants it, I will be afraid of that man. But if that man says, "Why are you afraid? I do not want anything." I know all that is mine is safe and secure from him. Since he has no desires – not for things, people, or even his own body – he has no worry about their fulfilment. No desire hence, no fear.

Since he has no desire and so no one need fear him. Once when Lord Nārāyaṇa was in meditation, Indra, the King of heaven, got worried, as he was attached to his reign and his kingdom of heaven. So, wanting to protect these, he sent the God of love and desire Kāmadeva and his denizens apsarās to distract Him. But when they went before the Lord, He laughed, and a beautiful apsarā came out of Him. The Lord said, "Give her to Indra as a present from Me."

The sannyāsī becomes fearless through Self-knowledge, he gives fearlessness to others by imparting Self-knowledge. Self-knowledge is the knowledge of oneness, of one's true Self. There can be fear only where there is a sense of otherness. If I am that one Truth which is one and the only one (non-dual), that is, I alone exist, what and whom should I fear? Striving for this state of being is called graceful living.

Song of the Enlightened

The sannyāsī, or Enlightened person, of whom Ādi Śaṅkara speaks, is also called a bhikṣu.

Bhikṣu-gītā or the 'Song of the Bhikṣu', is found in *Śrīmad Bhāgavatam.* In this scripture, there is a dialogue between Lord Kṛṣṇa and Uddhava. Uddhava says, "My Lord, You always advise that we must practise equipoise of mind, whether there is honour or dishonour, praise or censure. But O Lord, sometimes when people speak, flowers issue from their mouths. At other times, only arrows fly, and such words pierce the heart. Physical wounds heal,

but the wounds of such sharp words do not. And when such words are spoken by near and dear ones, it is so much more difficult to bear!"

If someone told me, "Swamiji, a man in Timbuktu was criticizing you," would I care?

But if someone cautions me, "Do you know what your disciple was saying?", immediately I want to hear more! We get lot of joy from our near and dear ones, but also maximum sorrow. Someone said, 'In politics, your enemy cannot harm you, but your friends will kill you.'

So how does one keep the mind calm, cool and collected? There is story in the Purāṇas. In Ujjain, there was a rich Brāhmaṇa. Generally, Brāhmaṇas are not rich, but this one was. He was very very miserly, neither spending money on himself nor on anyone else. One could take his skin, but not his money![1] He was also highly temperamental and arrogant. Anyone and everyone who had to deal with him, including his family, was very unhappy with him.

Once, some people wanting to build a community swimming pool approached him for a donation. He gave them a bucket of water – that was his contribution! Because he had money, no one spoke against him in public.

---

1 चमड़ी जाये पर दमड़ी न जाए।

Then, one day, the stock market crashed. And he lost everything! Thereafter, no one cared for him; no one asked about him; everyone ignored him totally. Pained through these hard times, he sadly went away from his town to a nearby solitary place. Surprisingly, perhaps because of some good actions done in an earlier life, or solely by God's grace, a complete transformation took place in him. Suddenly, He began thinking about the kind of life he had been living. When a person starts thinking in the right direction and makes Realization his goal, in due time, he becomes Enlightened. And this is exactly what happened to this Brāhmaṇa. He became a bhikṣu!

We all get surprises in life. This is one thing I have learnt from direct experience. And even though I have prepared myself for all surprises, pleasant and unpleasant, where the surprise will come from, is always a surprise!

One day, the bhikṣu entered his old town again. Seeing him with a stick (daṇḍa) and a

begging bowl (kamaṇḍalu) in his hands, some who did not know him started making fun of him. Many who knew him tauntingly said,

"Oh! You have come back as a great monk!"[1] They called him a hoax, and said, "We know what kind of person you really are!" They abused him verbally, took away his daṇḍa and kamaṇḍalu, beat him with sticks when he sat for his japa, and spat on him.

But he was totally silent and absolutely unperturbed. He had reached that state. In fact, he sang a song for them. Although all were bent on making him miserable, he joyously sang his song.

Know that peace of mind is the most precious wealth. We do not part with, sell, or easily give away objects that we believe are precious, or those for which we have sentimental value. Not even in tough financial times do we easily consider selling what is precious to us. So, the Enlightened man says, "My peace of mind is my greatest wealth. You are trying to destroy it by spitting at me or by scolding me. But you will have to work a little harder, for, it will not go away just like that!"

---

[1] आ गये बड़े सन्यासी बनकर

Conquer the Mind

The Brāhmaṇa said, "People, deities, the body, planets, actions, or time – none of these are the cause of my joy and sorrow. The mind alone is said to be the cause of saṁsāra."[1]

The Enlightened Brāhmaṇa says people are not the cause of his joy or sorrow; neither is God, nor are deities like Indra, Varuṇa, Kubera, nor the 33 crores of deities. The wise man knows that even his physical body can give him neither joy nor sorrow. The planets and their positions nor the constellation, nothing can give him joy or sorrow. Not even people – though they may try! Someone may try to annoy me, but whether I get annoyed or not depends on me alone.

People try to change us and we also try to change them. We think that our joy will come from getting what we want, seeing what we like or hearing what we desire. Some people are so

---

[1] नायं जनो मे सुखदुःखहेतुर्न देवताऽऽत्मा ग्रहकर्मकालाः ।
मनः परं कारणमामनन्ति संसारचक्रं परिवर्तयेद् यत् ॥
– श्रीमद्-भागवत-११·२३·४३

lazy that we cannot make them do anything! Try. Sometimes children play 'School'. Even in this game, one lazy boy said, "Let's play 'Holiday' instead. School is closed!"

When we want to change people so that they become and act as we like, sometimes we do it under the righteous shield of social service. But in this world, we have to learn and accept that there are some people who refuse to be happy – just as there are some who refuse to be sorrowful.

When the body is suffering, it can be very painful. Even the tough ones are unable to bear it.[1] But being happy or unhappy because of it is a different matter altogether. Someone may have cancer. So many Mahātmās also went through similar physical diseases. Yet they thought, 'Ha! It is there. So what!' Because of earlier karmas, certain situations may arise. People, devatās, planets, and even our physical body are capable of creating situations that can make us happy or unhappy – but that is

possible only if we choose to be influenced by them, if we choose to become happy or unhappy because of them. It is always solely our own choice.

1 अच्छे अच्छे को रुला देता है।

Different phases come in our life. We all have bad times also. So who creates all the joys and sorrows? All the Mahātmās and scriptures say, 'It is all only a play of the mind.' It is because of the mind that the wheel of saṁsāra moves. The mind gives value to certain things and beings, and according to these personal valuations, we choose to become happy or unhappy. We overreact to the smallest of things. If we get invited for a grand wedding, we consider it prestigious and boast about it. If we are not invited, we throw a tantrum. In fact, we could instead consider it fortunate that we got saved from the trouble of buying gifts and new outfits! Thus, the wise say we must conquer our own mind.

'Conquer the mind' means purify the mind. The best way to purify the mind is to always remember the Lord or of the goal of Realization, and to absorb the mind in that alone. When this happens, the mind becomes divine (Paramātma-svarūpa). Lord Kṛṣṇa says, "When the mind keeps brooding over sense objects and pleasures, it gets attached to them.

But when the same mind meditates on Me, it becomes one with Me." Therefore, the bhikṣu refuses to get bothered or angry by what people do or don't do. His only goal is to cross over the ocean of saṁsāra by being devoted to the lotus feet of the Lord. The devotee knows that whatever is to happen will happen anyway, so he does not mind what anyone says. He simply sings his song of Realization.

A Life Fulfilled

A devotee named Jaswant lived in Maharashtra. Later, he came to be known as Jani Jaswant. It is said that some relatives and ministers were jealous of him, so they made false allegations against him to the king. Without making proper inquiries, the king ordered that he should be thrown into a dry well. Jaswant was a devotee of Lord Rāma. Even in the well, he continued singing the Lord's name. The Lord rescued him and saw to it that no harm came to him. The king realized his mistake and fell at Jaswant's feet. Jaswant wrote and sang, 'As the Lord lifted Mount Meru by becoming a tortoise (kūrma) during the churning of the Milky Ocean, so too, He has saved me now.'

Thus, graceful ageing is to go through various stages of life – while growing in love for the Lord and remaining focused on the final goal of Realization. We should live a saṁskāra-yukta anuśāsanam in brahmacarya āśrama, vicāra-yukta ācaraṇam in gṛhastha āśrama, vairāgya-yukta adhyayanam in vānaprastha āśrama, and bhakti-yukta Paramātma-ramaṇam in sannyāsa āśrama. Our life then becomes full and complete with the ultimate peace and freedom of divine oneness.

OM

TRANSLITERATIONS OF FOOTNOTES

Page No.

1 *yadṛcchā-lābha-santuṣṭah... – Bhagavad-gītā-4.22* 20

1 *tadha tadvanaṁ nāma tadvanamītyupāsitavyaṁ...*
– Kenopaniṣad-4.6 21

1 *bramhaṇi carati iti* 22

2 *...sarvāṇi bhūtāni-saṁvañchanti. – Kenopaniṣad-4.6* 22

1 *amara vaha deśavā jahāṁ se āyo – Santa Kabīra* 24

1 *kāju hamāra tāsu hita hoī.*
– Śrīrāmacaritamānasa-6.16.4 27

2 *satyān-na pramaditavyam.*
– Taittirīya-upaniṣad-1.11.1 28

1 *vedo nityam-adhīyatāṁ... – Sādhanā Pañcakam-1* 35

1 *satyān-na pramaditavyam, dharmān-na pramaditavyam*
– Taittirīya-upaniṣad-1.11.1 37

1 *jagat guruḥ yasya saḥ jagadguruḥ.* 39

1 *dharmo rakṣati rakṣitaḥ – Manu Smṛti-8.15* 45

1 *...śiṣyaste'haṁ śādhi māṁ tvāṁ prapannam.*
– Bhagavad-gītā-2.7 47

1 *atithi devo bhava.* 55

1 *yat-karoṣi yadaśnāsi, yajjuhoṣi dadāsi yat,*
yattapasyasi kaunteya tatkuruṣra madarpaṇam.
– Bhagavad-gītā-9.27 59

1 *svakarmaṇā tam-abhyarcya siddhiṁ vindati mānavaḥ.*
– Bhagavad-gītā-18.46 60
